Serge Prengel

Commitment Phobia Workbook

How To Overcome
Fear Of Commitment

2nd Edition

Pausefully

Published by Pausefully, New York, NY.

Library of Congress Control Number: 2010900270

ISBN: 978-1-892482-30-3

Contents

Introduction

About this book

This is not a typical self-help book. Actually, don't even think of this as a book!

A book usually contains a lot of text. Reading is a fairly passive process. In contrast, this *workbook* is designed to get you actively involved.

You will notice quite a few charts, as well as spaces for *you to write* your answers to questions the workbook asks you.

First, a few words about the charts.

You may find them a bit puzzling at first. This is not the way you are accustomed to receive information, especially if this information is about the emotional side of life.

I am using flow charts because they prod you to be actively involved in the process.

The flow charts outline a process of self-exploration.
- You follow the arrows that correspond to your answers.
- At the end of the trail, you find a page number.
- Go to that page.

4

About commitment phobia

I want to make it clear that I am not using "phobia" as a diagnosis, with a medical or mental health connotation.

I am using the word in its colloquial meaning – the same way that we colloquially talk about being "paranoid", which has nothing to do with the psychiatric diagnosis of paranoia.

When I talk about commitment phobia, I am not talking about a psychiatric disorder. I am simply referring to people who are afraid of committing to relationships.

About your situation

I'll start with a question:
"What's wrong with not wanting to commit?"

There's nothing inherently wrong in not wanting to commit. Except, of course, if what's happening is you'd like to commit, but just can't seem to be able to.

Or if you don't want to commit, but your partner really wants you to. In which case, I don't presume that one of you is right, and the other wrong. I just note that there is a conflict.

So I'll start by asking you what you want.

Let's imagine that the two of you are sitting in the two chairs you see next page, and that you're having a conversation …

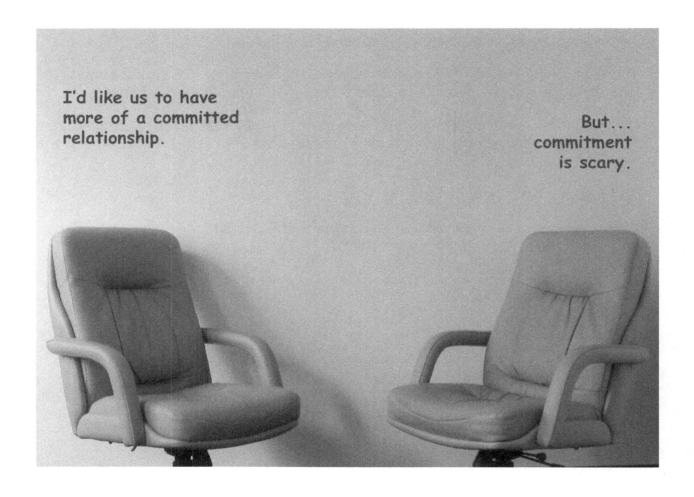

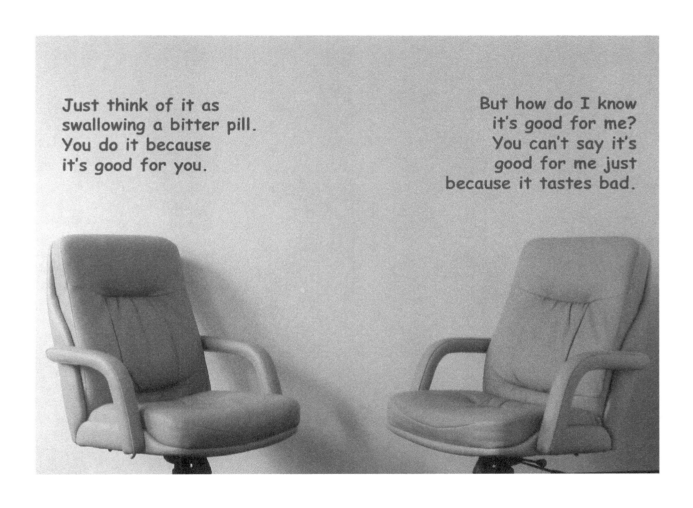

Just think of it as
swallowing a bitter pill.
You do it because
it's good for you.

But how do I know
it's good for me?
You can't say it's
good for me just
because it tastes bad.

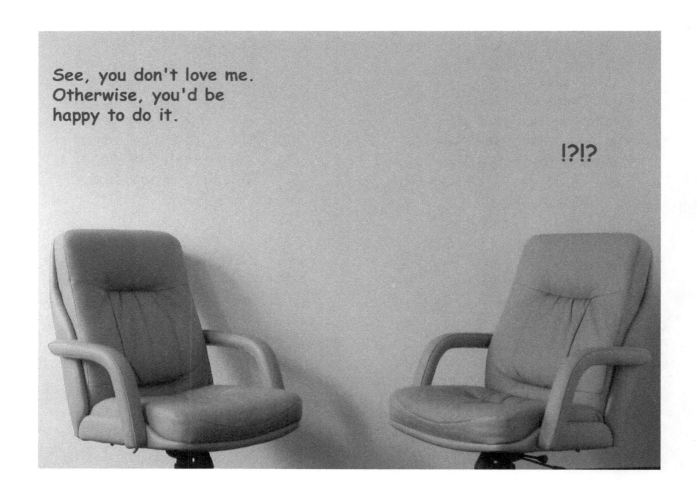

The result:
Each of you feels very misunderstood and very alone.

So let's stop the dialogue for the time being.

Let each of you go on a journey of your own.

I'll start by asking which chair you're sitting in – whether you are the commitment-phobe, or the partner of the commitment-phobe. And I'll ask you to go to the section of the book that is written for you.

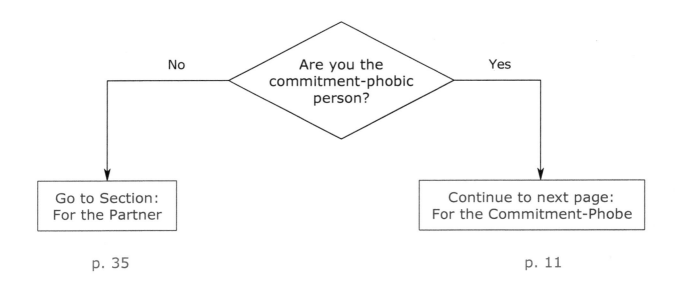

| No | Are you the commitment-phobic person? | Yes |

| Go to Section:
For the Partner | Continue to next page:
For the Commitment-Phobe |

p. 35   p. 11

For the Commitment-Phobe

If you're afraid of commitment, this fear is not strange.

"Commitment": the word itself can be scary. After all, just think of some of the phrases that go with "commitment", such as "being committed to custody", or "being committed to an insane asylum". They're about losing your freedom in a pretty drastic way.

The dictionary defines commitment as *"being bound emotionally or intellectually to a course of action or to another person(s)"*. It's understandable that you might feel some reluctance at the thought of "being bound".

Instead of swallowing a bitter pill "because it's good for you", let's try and explore things from your point of view.

You're feeling a lot of pressure – from your partner, and maybe also from a little voice inside. You hear that your unwillingness to commit is hurtful to your partner... that you're selfish or immature. You feel that you don't have space to hear yourself think.

You say that you need time... that you need space. Let's make time and space to understand how you feel.

14

First, let's take an honest look at why you're reading this book, and what you want to get out of it.
In the chart below, each "diamond" asks you a question. Follow the "yes" or "no" arrows.

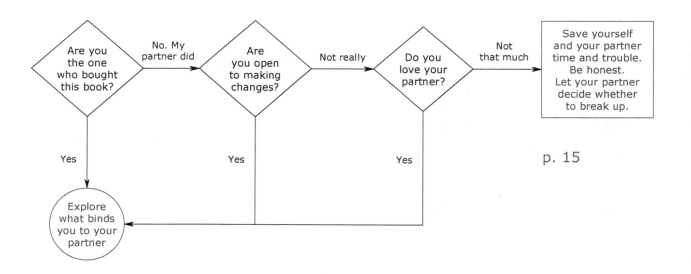

p. 15

p. 16

Save yourself and your partner time and trouble: Be honest.

If you're here, it's because you answered that you don't love your partner that much. You're happy enough to be in the relationship as it is, but you have no intention make this relationship significantly deeper than it is.

This would be OK if your partner were on the same wavelength.
Chances are this is not the case: what's probably happening is that your partner wants to deepen the relationship. And your partner believes that you might eventually be amenable to it.

Why does your partner believe this? Is it just that your partner is deluded? Is it possible that, in order to avoid conflict, you're implying that you may eventually be open to a more committed relationship?

In any case, I'd suggest you be honest. Save yourself and your partner a lot of time and trouble. Tell your partner where you stand... and let your partner decide whether (or when) to break up.

Note:

If the perspective of a breakup makes you feel less certain about where you stand, and you feel more open to exploring deepening your commitment, continue this process.

If you don't feel bad about breaking up, stop here.
And go tell your partner that you're breaking up.

Explore what binds you to your partner

Instead of swallowing a bitter pill "because it's good for you", ask yourself:
"What's in this for me?"

More specifically:
"What is it that I really value in this relationship?"

What if you're thinking: "There's nothing I really value"?
Come on, be real. Make an effort to remember the good times.

If you see yourself starting to come up with a "laundry list" of good things... let go
of that. Close your eyes. Try to recapture ONE good moment of the relationship.
Visualize this moment. Explore it. Get into the feelings of that moment. Let yourself
resonate with them, in a powerful, emotional way.

Keep this picture in your mind's eye. Then describe it.

WRITE HERE:

How do you feel as you contemplate this vivid picture?

For instance:
Does it make you feel happy? Or unhappy? Or...?
Do you start to have thoughts?

How do you feel about not committing to your partner?
- I feel OK about that. I need the time and space.
- I feel some guilt ("It's unfair to my partner")
- I feel some shame ("I should be more mature")
- I feel genuinely puzzled by the fact that I love my partner, yet I keep resisting commitment.

WRITE HERE:

What are you going to do with these feelings?

Follow the arrows in the flowchart:

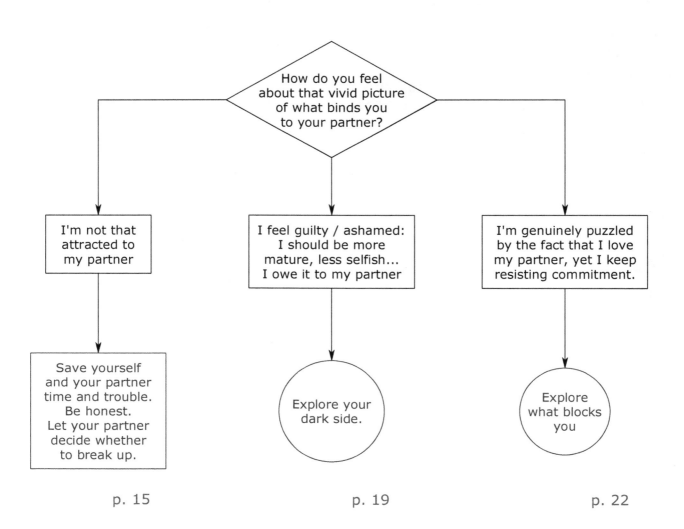

How do you feel about that vivid picture of what binds you to your partner?

I'm not that attracted to my partner

I feel guilty / ashamed: I should be more mature, less selfish... I owe it to my partner

I'm genuinely puzzled by the fact that I love my partner, yet I keep resisting commitment.

Save yourself and your partner time and trouble. Be honest. Let your partner decide whether to break up.

Explore your dark side.

Explore what blocks you

p. 15

p. 19

p. 22

Explore your Dark Side:

You contemplate that vivid picture of what binds you to your partner, and then you ask yourself how you feel about that. What comes up for you is mostly feelings of guilt or shame. For instance: "I should be more considerate to my partner", or "I'm really selfish" or "I should be more mature"... those kinds of things...

Now, it is quite honorable of you to want to be a better person. On the other hand, when we think in terms of "shoulds", there is some cause to be suspicious. "I should" often implies "... but I don't really want to".

So let's take time to explore the Dark Side. Ask yourself: What if there is actually a part of me that wants the exact opposite of the "shoulds"?

Use the next page to give a voice to this Dark Side – the part of you that you may judge as selfish, immature, small-minded.

Remember:
This is not about encouraging you to follow your basest instincts. This exercise is just meant to help you be more aware of the pull that the Dark Side can exert. As you get more aware of it, you have more power to consciously decide what kind of balance you will strike between these impulses and your "shoulds".

Give voice to your Dark Side - - the part of you that stands for the exact opposite of all the "shoulds" you are trying to follow.

WRITE HERE

Then go next page to see where this leads you.

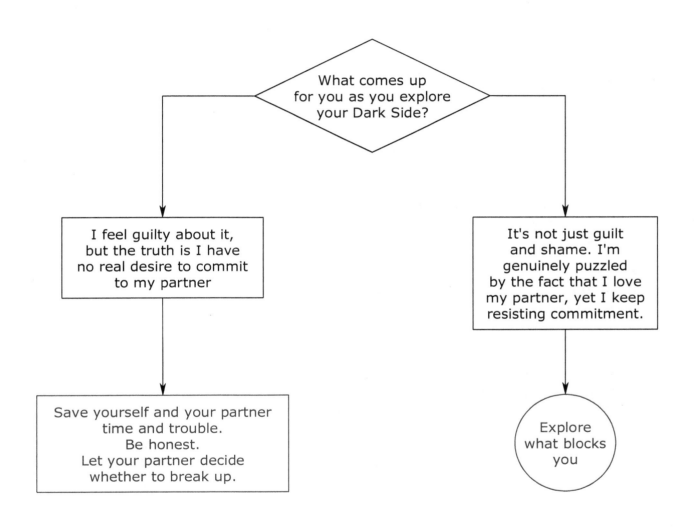

Explore what blocks you:
Visit your fear of commitment

Think again about that vivid picture of what attracts you to your partner. Think of this picture as the end of a path that you are traveling.

Ask yourself:
"What is it that stands between me and this picture?"

Take your time.
This is about letting yourself hear all the things that stand between you and that vivid picture of happiness... all the things that prevent you from yielding to the attraction... jumping in... and committing to the relationship.

Remember, all of this is happening in the privacy of your own mind. You do not have to reveal any of what you see to anybody else. You don't even have to write it here if you don't want to.
If you feel defensive, you're defending against nothing else than your own judgments of yourself.

By the way, this is not about criticizing yourself, either ("what stands between me and this picture of happiness is that I'm immature and selfish"). No judgments. Just facts or feelings.

Stay simple, literal even. Be open that the answer may very well not be what you (or your partner) has been re-hashing. Maybe it is so simple that it sounds silly. It's OK. Be open to what comes up for you.

What is between you and this vivid picture of what attracts you to your partner?

Here again, stay simple.

If you see yourself coming up with a lot of reasons, take a deep breath. It's not about analyzing, even less so about criticizing yourself.

It's about getting in touch with the fear that is between you and something you value.

Facts. Feelings. Fears...
What is between you and this vivid picture?

WRITE HERE

Let's now see how what you wrote fits into the following categories:

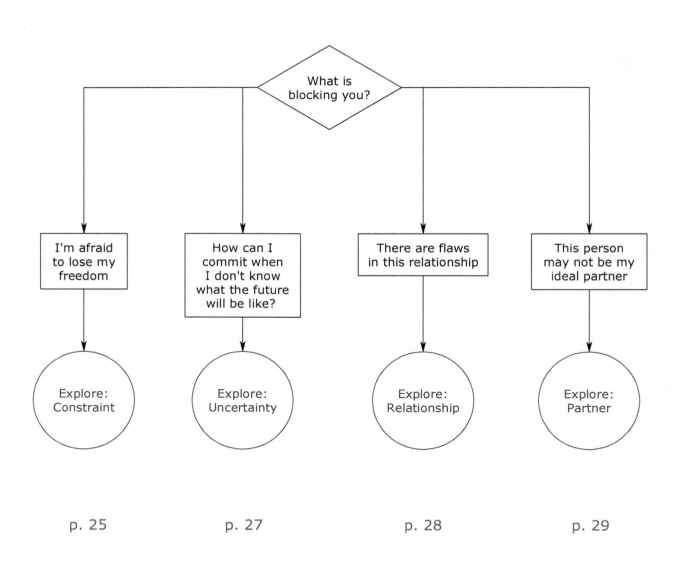

p. 25   p. 27   p. 28   p. 29

The fear:

"Being committed feels like losing my freedom."

The reality behind the fear:

When you're in a couple, you have to take into consideration the needs and wants of your partner. This can be really difficult if the two of you do not handle conflict well. For instance:
- you fight about many decisions, big and small
- or: you rarely if ever fight, but avoid the difficult decisions
- or: one or both of you give in without really meaning to, which fosters resentment

What to do about it:

Improve your conflict resolution skills:
- practice active listening
- discuss options instead of digging yourselves into trenches

Set a timeline for yourself:
Resolve to review how you feel about your fear in one month, two months, three months.

At those times, ask yourself whether you feel "closer", "less close", or "about the same" toward making a commitment to your partner.

If your fears are still very strong, it may be that:
- the two of you are still not very good at dealing with conflicts, and this is justifiably scaring you,
- or: your fears are so strong that they are not based on the reality of your situation.

Explore: Uncertainty

The fear:

"How can I commit when I don't know what the future will be like?"

The reality behind the fear:

It is true that you don't know for sure that your feelings for your partner won't change, or that circumstances won't change. However, the problem of making decisions in the face of uncertainty is not unique to relationships. We constantly have to do so: e.g. deciding what to study, what field to work in, where to live, etc...

What to do about it:

Right now, you feel very alone with your fear: it feels like this is the kind of decision you have to make all alone, because you can't really trust that your partner's interest and yours coincide. This is the opposite of what it would be like to be in a supportive relationship – one in which making difficult decisions is made easier by the love and support of your partner.

Give yourself a trial period of one, two, three months. See what it would feel like to actually experience a loving, supportive relationship. During this period, pay attention to moments when you feel you are facing the world alone, and do your best to share the situation with your partner. Practice being there for each other.

If your fears are still very strong, it may be that:
- the two of you need to improve your ability to be supportive to each other,
- or: your fears are so strong that they are not based on the reality of your situation.

Explore: Relationship

The fear:

"There are flaws in this relationship."

The reality behind the fear:

There may be quite a few conflicts between you and your partner. Having conflicts is not necessarily a sign that this is a bad relationship (actually, having no conflict whatsoever could be more worrisome). It's not the conflicts, it's how you handle them.

What to do about it:

Go beyond the generalities ("there are problems in this relationship"). Identify the problems, and deal with them:
- practice active listening
- discuss options instead of digging yourselves into trenches

Review how you feel about the relationship in one month, two months, three months.

Then ask yourself whether the relationship problems still feeling as intractable, or significantly less so.

Explore: Partner

The fear:

"This person may not be my ideal partner."

The reality behind the fear:

There may be quite a few discrepancies between your actual partner and what an ideal partner would be. Then again, we live in an imperfect world, and few things are ideal. The issue is whether what draws you to your partner outweighs what pulls you apart.

What to do about it:

Ask yourself whether there are specific things that lead you to think your partner may not be the ideal partner for you... or whether this feeling is more about your fear of missing out on a possibly better opportunity.
The chart next page outlines a thought process you can follow to unravel these options.

What to do if you fear your partner may not be the ideal partner for you:

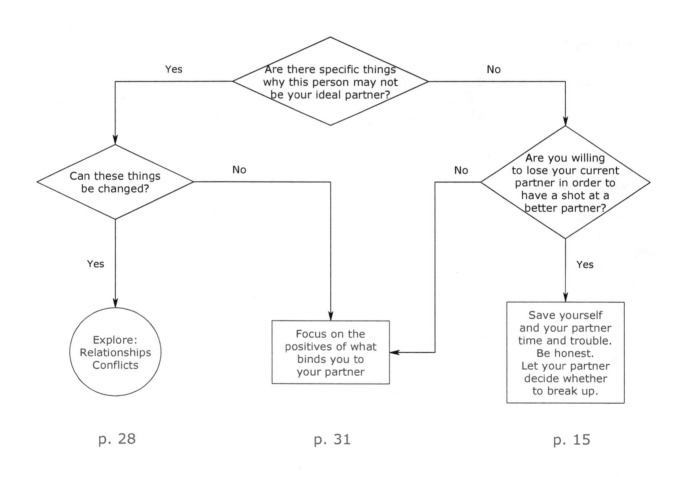

Are there specific things why this person may not be your ideal partner?

Yes

No

Can these things be changed?

No

Are you willing to lose your current partner in order to have a shot at a better partner?

No

Yes

Yes

Explore: Relationships Conflicts

Focus on the positives of what binds you to your partner

Save yourself and your partner time and trouble. Be honest. Let your partner decide whether to break up.

p. 28

p. 31

p. 15

Can you focus on the positive?

You are in the heart of your ambivalence: You feel that this is not your ideal partner, but you are not willing to lose the relationship. It might feel safe to stay on the fence, but there is an emotional cost to living in ambivalence. Give yourself a chance to see what it might feel like to cross that line. Take some time to focus on the positives of the relationship. The negatives are still there. How does it feel to focus on what you like instead of what turns you off?

WRITE HERE: WHERE YOU'RE AT RIGHT NOW

THEN COME BACK TO THIS BOOK IN A WEEK (SEE NEXT PAGE).

A week later:

Start from the beginning, review what you had written. And then ask yourself some questions.

WRITE HERE HOW YOU FEEL WHEN YOU FOCUS ON THE POSITIVES OF BEING TOGETHER:

THEN GO TO THE NEXT PAGE:

What have you learned about yourself though this process?

WRITE HERE:

THEN GO TO THE NEXT PAGE

What are you resolving to do about the commitment issues that prompted you to read this?

WRITE HERE:

Then go to: What next: p. 47

For the Partner

of the Commitment-Phobe

A different perspective

When you started reading this book, you probably expect to find in it a passionate plea for commitment, and a sharp criticism of people who cannot or won't commit. So you may have been surprised when I asked, in the introduction: "What's wrong with not wanting to commit?"

I was intentionally provocative in order to make a point.

It is tempting to view the issue of commitment with a "right or wrong" approach. For instance: "It is wrong of my partner to be avoiding commitment". Or, in a different vein: "Is there something wrong with me that is causing my partner to avoid commitment?".

I prefer to think of commitment within the context of the relationship. The problem is when one partner wants more commitment, and the other doesn't.

Looking at it this way, it's not just about commitment, it's also about how you two, as a couple, are able to manage conflict. Look at it this way: if the relationship is to go on, and to become deeper, it's not going to be the fairy tale ending of "happy ever after". In real-life relationships – even very happy relationships – there are plenty of conflicts. What makes a relationship good is not the absence of conflict, it's your ability to deal with conflict.

Why am I saying this?

I would like you to adopt a different attitude toward this commitment issue.

Right now, the way you think of the issue is probably something like: "If only my partner would feel differently about commitment, we'd have cleared the last big hurdle toward happiness, and life would be so much easier from then on"... and you'd probably have some expectation of a rosy, conflict-free future.

Well, as I said above, there is no such thing. If your relationship deepens, your lives will be more intertwined, and therefore you will have more opportunities for conflict.

So the different attitude I am suggesting for you is:
"This struggle about commitment is a great opportunity for us to practice resolving difficult conflicts".

This is a way to see what's happening within a broader complex. The struggle you're having right now is part of what relationships are all about – struggling between being individuals and being a couple.

In practice, how is this going to be different from what you've been doing?

For one thing, I hope this broader perspective helps you relax some of the pressure that you may be putting on yourself and your partner. After all, if what's happening is part of the normal process of what relationships are all about, there is less of a need to be on "high alert" mode for dealing with it.

Relaxing the pressure means feeling less antagonistic.

What happens in a conflict situation (not just this one) is that you feel: "it's me against my partner". So you have the paradoxical situation that, on the one hand, you're trying to be more of a couple... and, on the other hand, you're experiencing this as a moment of being very alone, fighting against the person you want to be a couple with!

In other words, your challenge is to start to conceive of what's happening as something that involves both of you, as opposed to something that your partner perpetrates against you.

Does this mean that you essentially cave in to what your partner wants?

Not at all. Remember, I said this is part of dealing with the conflicts in a relationship, part of dealing with being individuals as well as members of a couple. Your goal is certainly not to lose yourself in order to have a relationship.

You can want what you want and be firm about it.

So, you'll say, what's different about what's happening now? I'm certainly not shy about asking my partner to commit!

The difference is in the style of the struggle.

The antagonistic struggle is a bit like the trench-warfare of World War One. Each partner is entrenched in their position and won't budge. You keep using heavy artillery against each other's position, in the hope that the other person will "see the light" and see the wisdom of your position.

In contrast, the approach I am suggesting is one in which, while you are clear about what you each want, you are also each willing to look at things within a broader perspective, and to look inside in order to re-examine your assumptions.

This workbook provides a structure for this process. Earlier in the book, there is a section for the commitment-phobe's process. This section is about your process.

What if your partner refuses to look inside, or, having looked inside, refuses to budge?

Then, as in any other conflict situation, it is up to you to draw the consequences. It may very well be that the best thing for you to do, at that point, is to end the relationship.

Well, you may say, if I'm going to end the relationship, what's the difference between what you're suggesting and what I was doing?

For one thing, the approach I am suggesting may be better suited to help you not have to end the relationship. After all, if you deal with this issue in a collaborative manner, as a training ground for dealing with future relationship conflicts, this may very well be what it takes to assuage the fears your partner may have about being in a relationship.

But, even if this fails, and you end the relationship... it will be in a different way. You will not be left with the feeling that "we had everything to be happy, but my partner was unwilling to commit". Instead, you will have experienced the situation as the tug-of-war of being unable to resolve conflict... which means you would probably not be able to resolve future conflicts in the relationship... and you have less to regret.

The following chart provides a framework to explore your perspective about the commitment issue. It asks you a few questions. Start from the question on the left, and follow the "yes" or "no" arrows.

The pages that follow the chart provide comments.

Questions to ask yourself

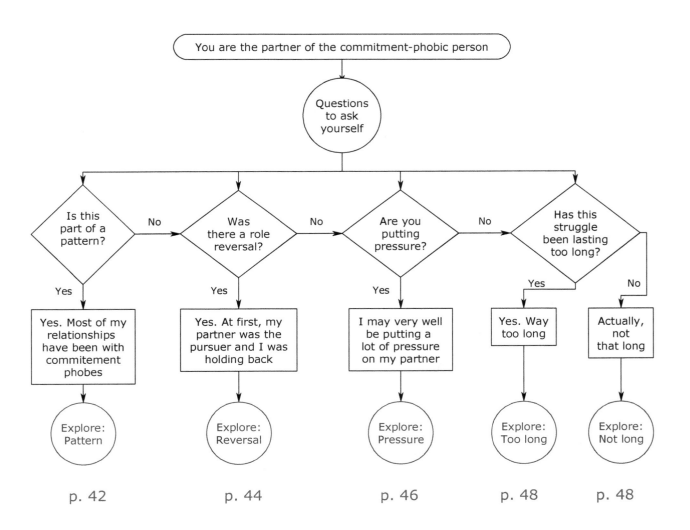

Explore: Pattern

"Is this part of a pattern?"

WRITE HERE

THEN LOOK AT NEXT PAGE

Explore: Pattern – cont'd

If you find that you've had a pattern of being in relationships with commitment-phobes, you may ask yourself how this came to happen, and what it might mean.

- For instance, is it possible that you too might be afraid of commitment? If so, this can lead you to approach discussions with your current partner in a different way (you would show more understanding for your partner's fears).

- Or is it that you hadn't really realized how you can get conned into believing your partners' promises that the situation could eventually evolve your way? You may now decide to be more assertive about what you want, and less patient…

Explore: Reversal

"Was there a role reversal? That is: was your partner the pursuer at the beginning of the relationship? Did things change when you shifted from being the reluctant one to being the pursuer?"

WRITE HERE

THEN LOOK AT NEXT PAGE

Thinking of what's happening now within the broader context of you and your partner switching roles as pursuer / pursued would help you see things in a different light.

As you remember being the reluctant one, you can have more of a sense of how your partner currently feels.

When you two talk about the issue, you can remind your partner that your partner has also experienced the position you're in now. Not only can you understand each other's current positions better, you can also explore what it is that caused the role reversal.

Explore: Pressure

"Are you putting a lot of pressure on your partner? On yourself?"

WRITE HERE

Explore: Pressure – cont'd

I discussed the issues about pressure in the introduction. I assumed that this was the norm rather than the exception in this kind of situation.

Having a broader perspective will help you reduce the pressure, and start to shift from experiencing this situation as one in which you're very alone, in fighting mode… to one in which the two of you are working in parallel to solve a couple conflict.

Explore: Lasting too long / not that long

"Has this struggle been lasting too long?"

WRITE HERE

THEN LOOK AT NEXT PAGE

Explore: Lasting too long / not that long – cont'd

This is not about having an objective, quantitative measurement of what "too long" or "not that long" means.

As you look at the situation within a broader perspective, you can get a sense of whether you're dealing with a longstanding, intractable conflict, or whether you're alarmed by the first signs of a possible conflict.

If you feel that this has been a long conflict, with no end in sight… it may very well be time for you to end the relationship. After all, this is not just about your partner not wanting to commit, this is also about your inability as a couple to resolve conflicts, which doesn't bode well for how you'd fare as a couple.

If, on the other hand, you realize it hasn't been going on for that long… then this realization can help you relax the pressure and approach this endeavor in a more collaborative and hopeful spirit.

What next?

For both the commitment-phobe *and* the partner

If you've come this far, it means you have ruled out ending the relationship. You've had this option earlier in the process, and it didn't feel right.

You may still feel quite ambivalent, but there is a difference. Instead of just staying entrenched on your positions, to commit or not to commit, you have broadened the discussion. You have started a process of understanding yourself better.

If you have shared some of this process with your partner, you have also started to understand each other better. If you have not shared this process, I would suggest you consider doing starting now.

Continue to share with your partner what both of you have found out about yourselves while using this book. Continue to be curious and interested in learning more about each other.

As you do, you will get better at finding ways to make room for the other's needs while also respecting your own. As opposed to an all-or-nothing approach, where one person wins and the other loses.

If you are able to keep doing this, chances are your relationship will strengthen, and you will want to be more committed to each other. Not from a sense of feeling trapped into it, but from a sense of appreciating being a couple who can deal with difficult issues together and learn from the experience.

About

Serge Prengel

"I have always been very interested in the creative process, at the individual level and in collaboration. Not as an object of academic study, but as a space I really like to live in.

"I think of coaching as a creative process in which both client and coach are engaged. Not that it's all fun and games, especially when we deal with deep-seated fears. But I find that keeping a connection to the creative side is a great resource to counterbalance the fears."

Active Pause website

http://activepause.com

Pausefully books

http://pausefully.com